Smart Animals

CHIMPANZEES

by Margaret Fetty

Consultant: Rebecca Gullott
Collection Manager, Mammals
The Maryland Zoo in Baltimore

BEARPORT
PUBLISHING COMPANY, INC.

Credits

Cover (center), Tim Davis/Corbis; Cover (background), Octavio Campos Salles/ istockphoto; Title Page, Tim Davis/Corbis; 4, Archive of University Nevada Reno; 5, H.S. Terrace/Animals Animals, Earth Scenes; 6, H.S. Terrace/Animals Animals, Earth Scenes; 7, Bruce Davidson/Nature Picture Library; 8, Dave Herring; 9, OSF/Clive Bromhall/Animals Animals, Earth Scenes; 10, OSF/Clive Bromhall/Animals Animals, Earth Scenes; 11, Anup Shah/Nature Picture Library; 12, Frans Lanting/Minden Picture; 13, Great Ape Trust of Iowa; 14, Courtesy of Dr. Sue Savage-Rumbaugh, Great Ape Trust of Iowa; 15, Courtesy of Dr. Sue Savage-Rumbaugh, Great Ape Trust of Iowa; 16, Tom McHugh/Photo Researchers; 17(l) Karl Ammann/Nature Picture Library; 17(r), Michael Nichols/National Geographic; 18, SuperStock; 19, SuperStock; 20, Dave Herring; 21, Primate Research Institute, Kyoto University; 22, Jim Caldwell/Suncoast Primate Sanctuary, Inc.; 23, Jim Caldwell/Suncoast Primate Sanctuary, Inc.; 24, Karl Ammann/ Nature Picture Library; 25, The Jane Goodall Institute, www.janegoodall.org; 26, Georg Gerster/Photo Researchers, Inc.; 27, Anup Shah/Nature Picture Library; 28, Michael Fay/National Geographic; 29, Chimpanzee Nikkie in Burgers' Zoo Arnhem, © Otto Adang.

Design and production by Dawn Beard Creative and Octavo Design and Production, Inc.

Library of Congress Cataloging-in-Publication Data

Fetty, Margaret.
  Chimpanzees / by Margaret Fetty.
    p. cm. — (Smart animals!)
  Includes bibliographical references and index.
  ISBN 1-59716-159-4 (library binding) — 1-59716-185-3 (pbk.)
  1. Chimpanzees—Juvenile literature. 2. Chimpanzees—Psychology—Juvenile literature.
I. Title. II. Series.

  QL737.P96F48 2006
  599.885—dc22

               2005026829

For more information, write to Bearport Publishing Company, Inc., 101 Fifth Avenue, Suite 6R, New York, New York 10003. Printed in the United States of America.

1 2 3 4 5 6 7 8 9 10

Contents

Signs of Language

Washoe (WAH-shoh) was born in Africa, but she grew up in Nevada. When she was about two years old, Washoe loved to get piggyback rides. She would tell the person who carried her which direction to go. Washoe couldn't use spoken words to tell the person, though. Washoe is a chimpanzee!

▲ **This is Washoe. She is the first non-human to learn a human language.**

So how does Washoe **communicate** with people? She uses her hands. Washoe learned **American Sign Language** (ASL), a language used by people who can't hear. Instead of speaking words, Washoe signs, or makes hand movements that stand for words.

Gorillas and orangutans have also been taught to use sign language.

▲ **This chimp is learning to sign the word for "eyes."**

5

New Names

Washoe began learning sign language in 1966. Other chimps have been taught to sign since then. Some of them know about 240 words. They can ask for food and drinks. When they see something they know, like a dog, they make the sign for it. One chimp even asked who was coming to play by signing "who play?"

▲ **Like Washoe, this chimp is learning sign language.**

Some scientists believe that chimps can communicate in sign language as well as a three- or four-year-old human child.

Sometimes, chimps combine words they know to name new things. One day, a chimp named Lucy was given watermelon to eat. She did not know the name of this fruit. So Lucy signed the words "drink fruit." Scientists agree that combining words shows that chimps are **intelligent**.

▲ **Chimps are one of the few animals who can recognize their reflections.**

Social Animals

Chimps are very **social** animals. In the wild, 40 to 60 chimps live together in one area. Chimps use their face, body, and sounds to tell other members in their **troop** how they are feeling.

Chimpanzees in the Wild

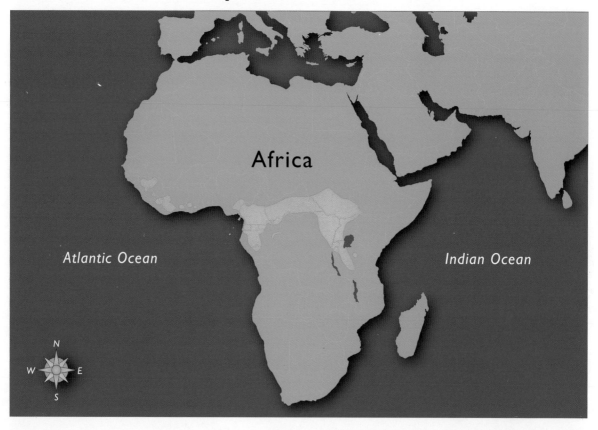

■ Range of chimpanzees

▲ **Chimpanzees in the wild are found only in Africa. They live in rain forests, grasslands, and dry savannahs.**

When chimps want to scare away other chimps, they open their mouths and scream loudly. They also raise the hair on their bodies to make themselves look bigger.

Scientists wondered if chimps who were taught sign language would use it to communicate with one another. Cameras were put in the area where Washoe and other chimps lived. The video showed that chimps really did sign to each other.

Chimps show their teeth when they are angry, nervous, or frightened.

Teaching Others

Older chimps in the wild teach younger chimps how to do different tasks, such as finding food or cracking open nuts. Would chimps that knew sign language be able to teach younger ones? Scientists wanted to find out. So they had Loulis (LOO-liss), a young chimp, live with Washoe.

▲ **This young chimp watches as an adult uses a stone to crack open a nut.**

Young chimpanzees learn from adults which foods are safe to eat and how to build nests for sleeping.

Shortly after Loulis arrived, Washoe signed "come baby" to the young chimp. Loulis jumped into her arms. Then, on the eighth day, Loulis made his first sign. He signed the name of the person who gave him breakfast. Loulis became the first non-human to learn a human language from another non-human!

▲ **A few chimps have been taught to use sign language to communicate with people. All chimps, however, use sounds such as grunts and barks to communicate with one another. This chimp is making a sound called a pant-hoot.**

Using a Keyboard

Signing isn't the only way chimps have learned to communicate. Dr. Duane Rumbaugh has taught them another way. He made a computer keyboard that has **symbols** on it. The symbols stand for words and things. For example, a "Y" shape means "yes." An up-and-down line means "raisin."

▲ **A chimp named Panbanisha learns symbols to use on a computer keyboard.**

A chimp named Lana learned to use the keyboard to communicate. She could press symbols in different orders to ask for things or answer questions. Lana could ask for food and drinks. She could also ask someone to come play with her.

▲ **Lana**

Chimps use their hands for walking. The skin on their knuckles gets tough, which can make it hard for them to sign. It is easier for chimps to press a symbol on a keyboard.

Tools Are the Key

Austin and Sherman lived in Georgia. These chimps were also taught to use a keyboard. They pressed symbols to name human **tools**, such as a key and a wrench. They also learned how to use these tools.

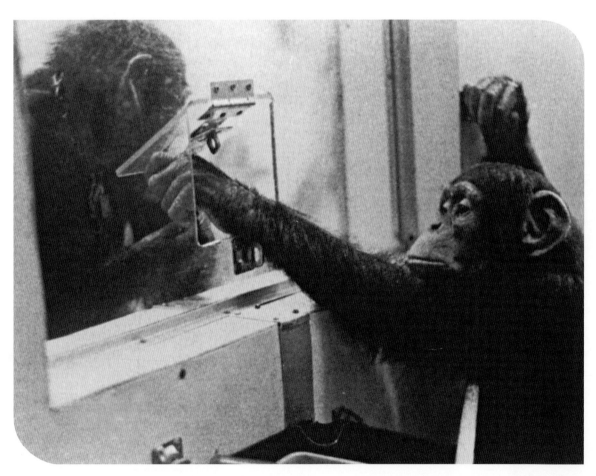

▲ **Austin passes a key through the window to Sherman.**

One day, scientists put some tools in Austin's room. In Sherman's room they placed a locked container with bananas inside. Austin could not see the container, so he did not know which tool would open it.

Sherman pressed "get key" on a keyboard. Austin saw the symbol light up. He passed a key to Sherman through a small window. Sherman used the key to open the container.

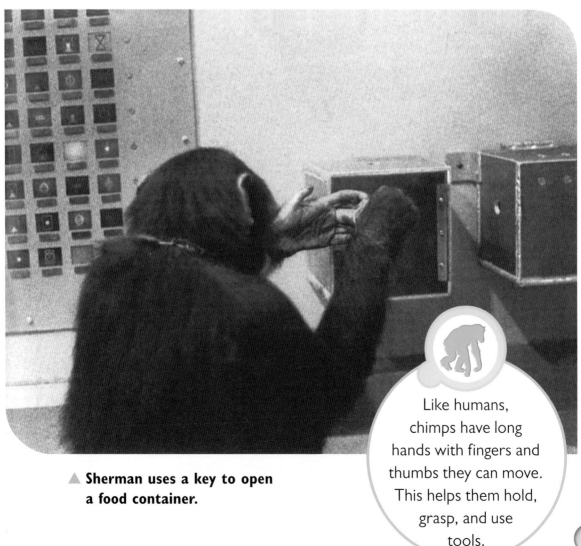

▲ **Sherman uses a key to open a food container.**

Like humans, chimps have long hands with fingers and thumbs they can move. This helps them hold, grasp, and use tools.

Tools in the Wild

Austin and Sherman learned to use human tools. Chimpanzees in the wild, however, make and use their own tools. For example, they strip leaves off a tree branch. Then, they use the branch to get **termites** out of the ground for a tasty treat.

Chimps use rocks, leaves, twigs, and tree branches as tools. Some chimps fold leaves and use them as tubes to get water into their mouths.

Some chimps along the African coast use rocks as tools. They return to one special place that has nut trees. They choose a flat rock. Then they crack open the nuts with another rock. Scientists say these actions show that chimps are smart. Not only are the chimps using tools, but they remember where the nut trees are.

▲ Chimps use twigs to get ants out of trees.

◄ This chimp uses a rock as a tool to crack open nuts.

Problem-Solving Chimps

Smart animals, like Austin and Sherman, find ways to solve problems. One scientist nailed some bananas to the ceiling of a chimp's room. He wanted to see how Sultan, the chimp, would find a way to get them.

Scientists believe that finding ways to solve problems is a sign of a smart animal.

▲ **Sultan**

Sultan jumped as high as he could, but it was no use. He couldn't reach the bananas. Sultan left the bananas alone for a while. Then suddenly, Sultan ran to a box that was in the room. He placed it on top of another box that was under the bananas. It was like a light bulb had gone off in his head. Standing on the boxes, Sultan was able to reach the fruit.

◀ **Sultan stacked boxes to reach the bananas.**

Math Problems

Humans often use math skills to solve problems. Ai (EYE) is a chimp who lives in Japan. She is smart enough to do math problems, too.

Ai sits in front of a computer. The screen shows a set of dots and two numbers. Ai counts the dots. Then she touches the number that shows the correct amount of dots!

Human and Chimp Brain Size

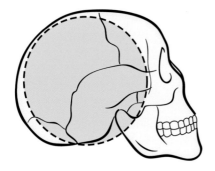
Human Skull and Brain

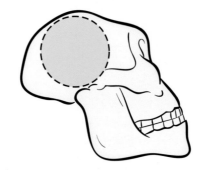
Chimpanzee Skull and Brain

Although chimps have large brains for their body size, humans have brains that are about twice as large.

Sometimes, Ai is given a bigger challenge. She is shown numbers on a computer screen. Scientists ask her to put the numbers in order. First, Ai touches the smallest number. Then, she touches the next biggest number. Ai puts the numbers in order from least to greatest.

▲ **Ai can put numbers in order from zero to nine.**

Picture Perfect

By learning and using math skills, Ai has proven how smart she is. However, Ai shows how intelligent she is in another way. Ai is an **artist**. She likes drawing pictures.

▲ **Sean is a chimp in Florida who loves to make art. Chimps who don't live in the wild are given many activities to do, including drawing, to keep them physically and mentally healthy.**

Congo was another chimp who liked to make pictures. He often used bright colors.

Congo was a neat artist. He never let the paint drip onto the paper or the table. Once Congo put his brush down, he was finished. Even if the painting was put back in front of him, he would not add anything to it.

▲ **A painting by Sean**

In 2005, three of Congo's paintings sold together for over $25,000!

Strong Feelings

Scientists have spent many years watching both wild and **captive** chimps. They have discovered that these smart animals have a wide range of **emotions**. Sometimes chimps can be serious. Sometimes they can be silly. Chimps can also have strong emotions, including **grief**.

▲ Jane Goodall, an English scientist, studied wild chimps in Africa for over 40 years.

Flo was a chimp who lived in Africa. When she died, her son, Flint, sat by her body and whimpered. Other chimps tried to **comfort** him. However, Flint moved away and started sitting alone. Soon, he stopped eating. Sadly, Flint died about three weeks later.

◀ **Flo and her son, Flint**

Jane Goodall was the first scientist to observe that wild chimps in Africa use tools. She also learned that the animals grieved when a member of their group died.

Protecting Chimpanzees

Chimps in the wild are very smart, but they are in danger of becoming **extinct**. Mother chimps are sometimes shot so that their babies can be sold as pets or used for entertainment. Some people hunt chimpanzees for food. Others cut down trees in the rain forests where chimps live. They want to use the trees for firewood and building. Some people want the land for making homes.

▲ **This forest in Africa was burned so that the land could be used for farming.**

Chimpanzees are an **endangered species**. Some laws have been passed to protect them. Yet more are still needed. Many people are working hard to make sure that these clever creatures continue to survive in the wild.

About 100 years ago, five million chimpanzees lived in Africa. Today, there are about 80,000 to 130,000.

Just the Facts

Chimpanzee

Height	3¼ – 5½ feet (1–2 m)
Weight	males: 90–120 pounds (41–54 kg) females: 60–110 pounds (27–50 kg)
Food	fruits, seeds, leaves, stems, termites, ants, and occasionally bush pigs and monkeys
Life Span	50–60 years
Habitat	tropical rain forests, grasslands, and savannahs in Africa

More Smart Chimpanzees

Yeroen and Nikkie are two male chimps living in a zoo in the Netherlands. After a fight, Yeroen began to walk with a limp. The scientists watched the chimp to see how badly he was hurt. They discovered that Yeroen only limped when Nikkie was nearby. Yeroen was just pretending to be hurt. He obviously did not want to fight with Nikkie again!

▲ **Nikkie**

Some chimps that live in areas surrounded by a high fence have found creative ways to get over them. One group of chimps took short sticks and pushed them into the holes in the fence. Then they used the sticks as steps to climb over the fence. Other chimps leaned a strong log against the fence and used it as a ladder to escape.

Glossary

American Sign Language
(uh-MER-uh-kuhn SINE LANG-gwij)
a language that is used instead of
spoken words; it is made up of hand
and body movements, as well as facial
expressions, and is often used by
people who can't hear

artist (AR-tist) someone who is
good at making art, such as a painter
or writer

captive (KAP-tiv) an animal that is
not living in its natural environment;
an animal that lives with and is cared
for by people

comfort (KUHM-fert) to give
support and strength

communicate
(kuh-MYOO-ni-kayt) to share
information, wants, needs, and
feelings

emotions (i-MOH-shuhnz) feelings

endangered species
(en-DAYN-jurd SPEE-sheez) a kind
of plant or animal that is in danger of
dying out

extinct (ek-STINGKT) a kind of
plant or animal that has died out;
there are no more alive on Earth

grief (GREEF) great sadness

intelligent (in-TEL-uh-juhnt) smart

social (SOH-shuhl) living in groups
and having contact with others

symbols (SIM-buhlz) things that
stand for or represent something else

termites (TUR-mites) an insect
that is like an ant and eats wood

tools (TOOLZ) objects that are
used to help do a job

troop (TROOP) a group of
chimpanzees who live together

Bibliography

de Waal, Frans. *Chimpanzee Politics: Power and Sex Among Apes,* rev. ed. Baltimore, MD: The Johns Hopkins University Press (1998).

Fouts, Roger, and Stephen Tukel Mills. *Next of Kin: My Conversations with Chimpanzees.* New York: HarperCollins (1998).

Gardner, R. Allen, Beatrix T. Gardner, and Thomas E. Van Cantfort. *Teaching Sign Language to Chimpanzees.* Albany, NY: State University of New York Press (1989).

Savage-Rumbaugh, Sue, and Roger Lewin. *Kanzi: The Ape at the Brink of the Human Mind.* New York: John Wiley & Sons (1994).

Read More

Banks, Martin. *Chimpanzee: Habitats, Life Cycles, Food Chains, Threats.* Austin, TX: Raintree (2000).

Goodall, Jane. *My Life with the Chimpanzees: The Fascinating Story of One of the World's Most Celebrated Naturalists,* rev. ed. New York: Aladdin (1996).

Martin, Patricia A. Fink. *Chimpanzees.* New York: Children's Press (2000).

Learn More Online

Visit these Web sites to learn more about chimpanzees:

www.chimp-ssp.org

www.discoverchimpanzees.org

www.friendsofwashoe.org

Index

About the Author

Margaret Fetty has been a writer and editor of educational materials for over 15 years. She has written 13 books for young readers.